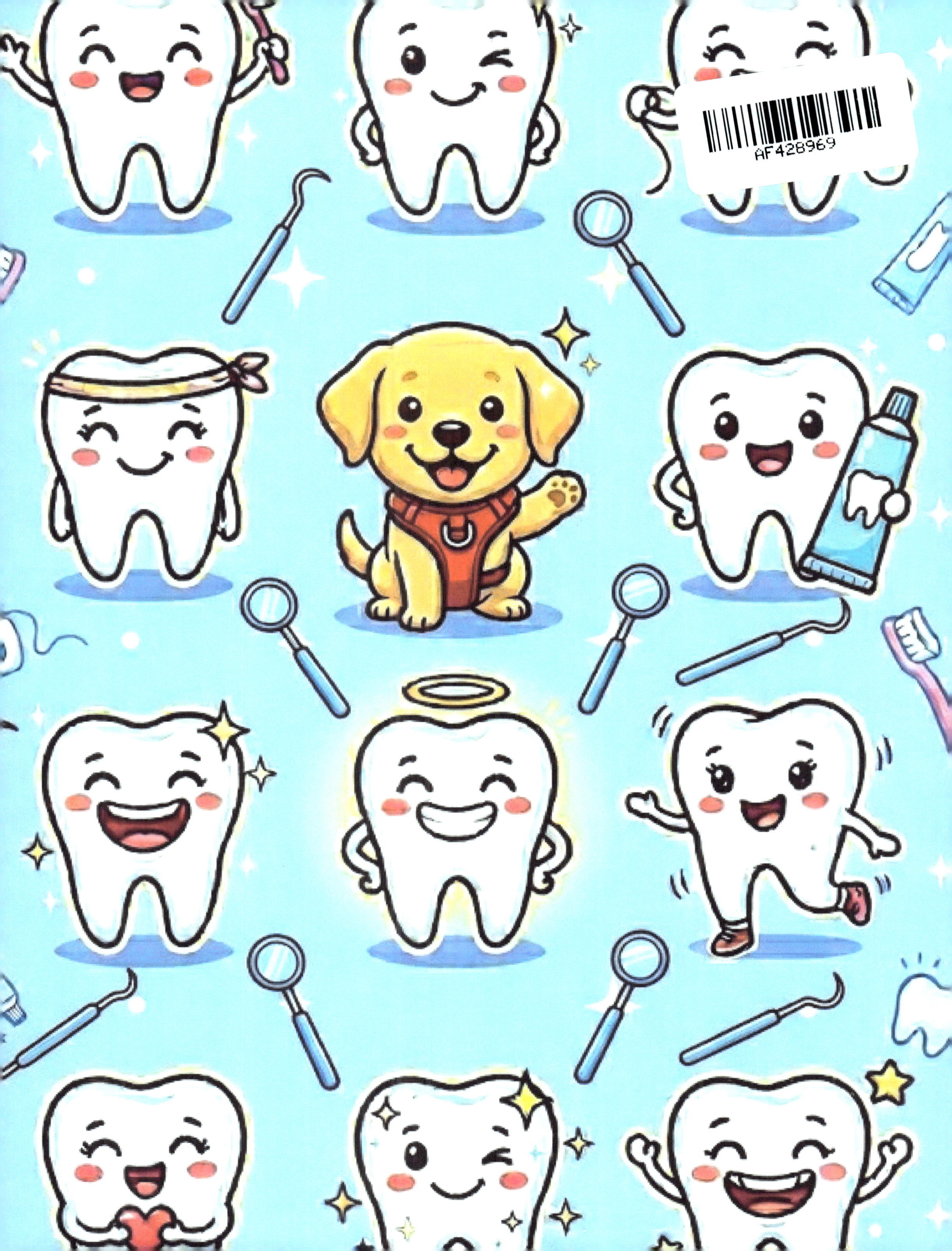
AF428969

To Jason and Brae,
Thank you for your love, support and believing in my ideas.

To Annie,
You are my sweet, furry child and the best co-worker in the
world. Thank you for being such a gentle soul. You were
born to do this. Everyone loves you.

To Dr. Lynelle Zabel D.D.S.
Thank you for allowing Annie to come into your office and
comfort everyone who walks through the doors of
Highlands Ranch Dental Care.

Annie the Therapy Dog
THERAPY DOG
Written by Lisa Trabert
Illustrated by Lisa Trabert

Annie was born in Colorado and has a
brother and sister that became service dogs.
Annie

We were so happy to bring our soft, little puppy home. We had lots of toys waiting for her. She had fun and played all day.

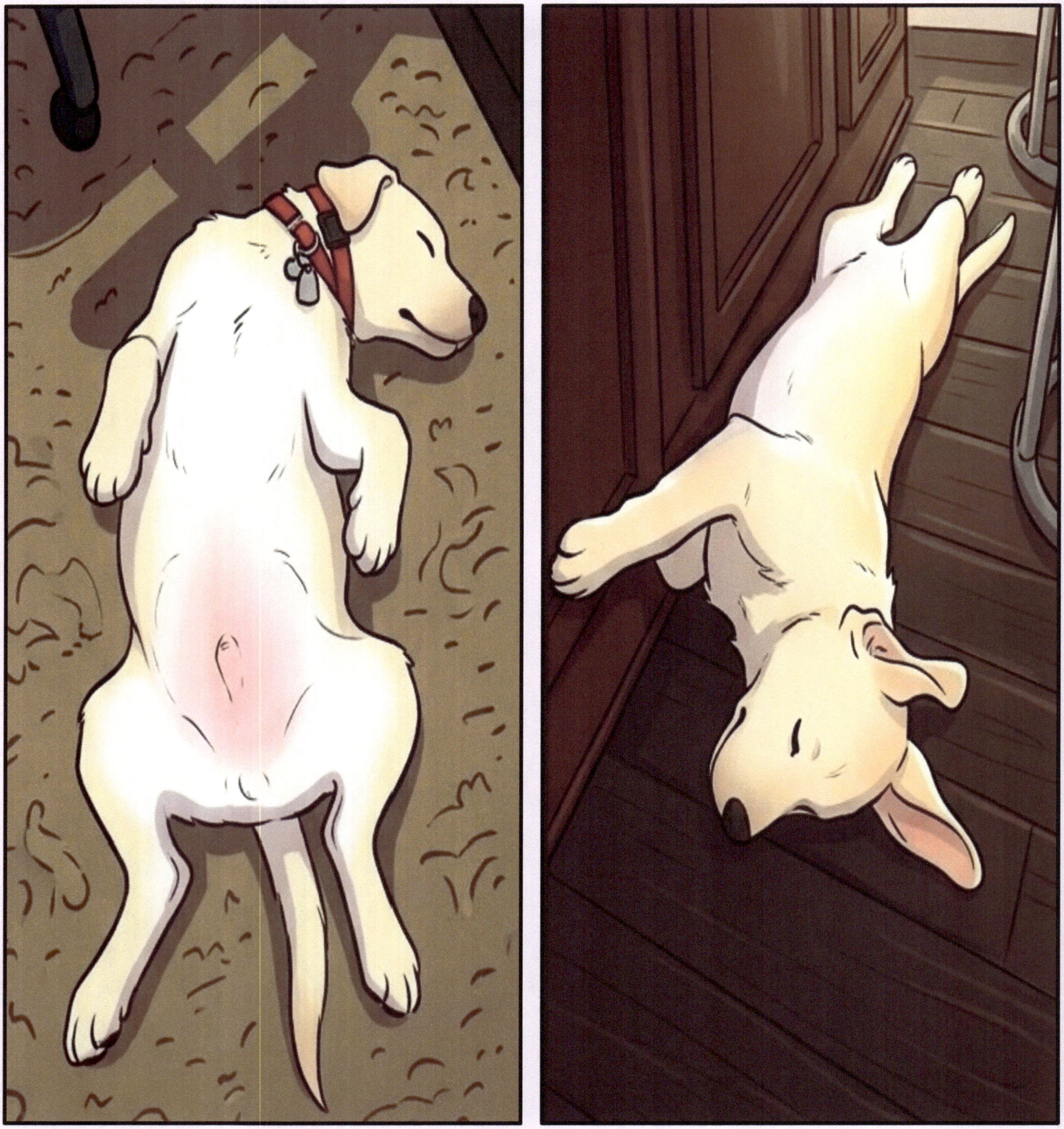

When Annie was tired, she liked to take
naps in silly spots and positions.

Annie is learning how to wear her new red puppy harness during walks in the park.
PARK
4

Annie was trained in doggy school to become a therapy dog and got her certificate when she graduated. She was now ready to help people!

Annie's handler, Lisa, took her to work in the dental office the next day. The patients and staff loved her.

Annie became part of the dental team and made lots of new friends with the people she works with.

Annie will gently hop into a patient's lap, and she feels like a warm comfort blanket.

Sometimes Annie will sit or lay next to
a patient like this person who is
getting an x-ray of their tooth.
9

Annie likes to gently hop up and snuggle with her patients in the dental chair. She makes people happy to come in and get their teeth worked on.

Annie helps patients in our dental office by greeting them with a warm, friendly hug.

If it's someone's birthday Annie will wear her birthday party hat. Annie loves birthday parties and, of course, birthday cake!

Annie will also dress-up as a tooth fairy on Halloween. Not all superheroes wear capes, some wear wings!

Annie loves getting hugs and lots
of love from children.

Annie also likes to watch children pick special toys from the treasure chest when their dental visit is done.

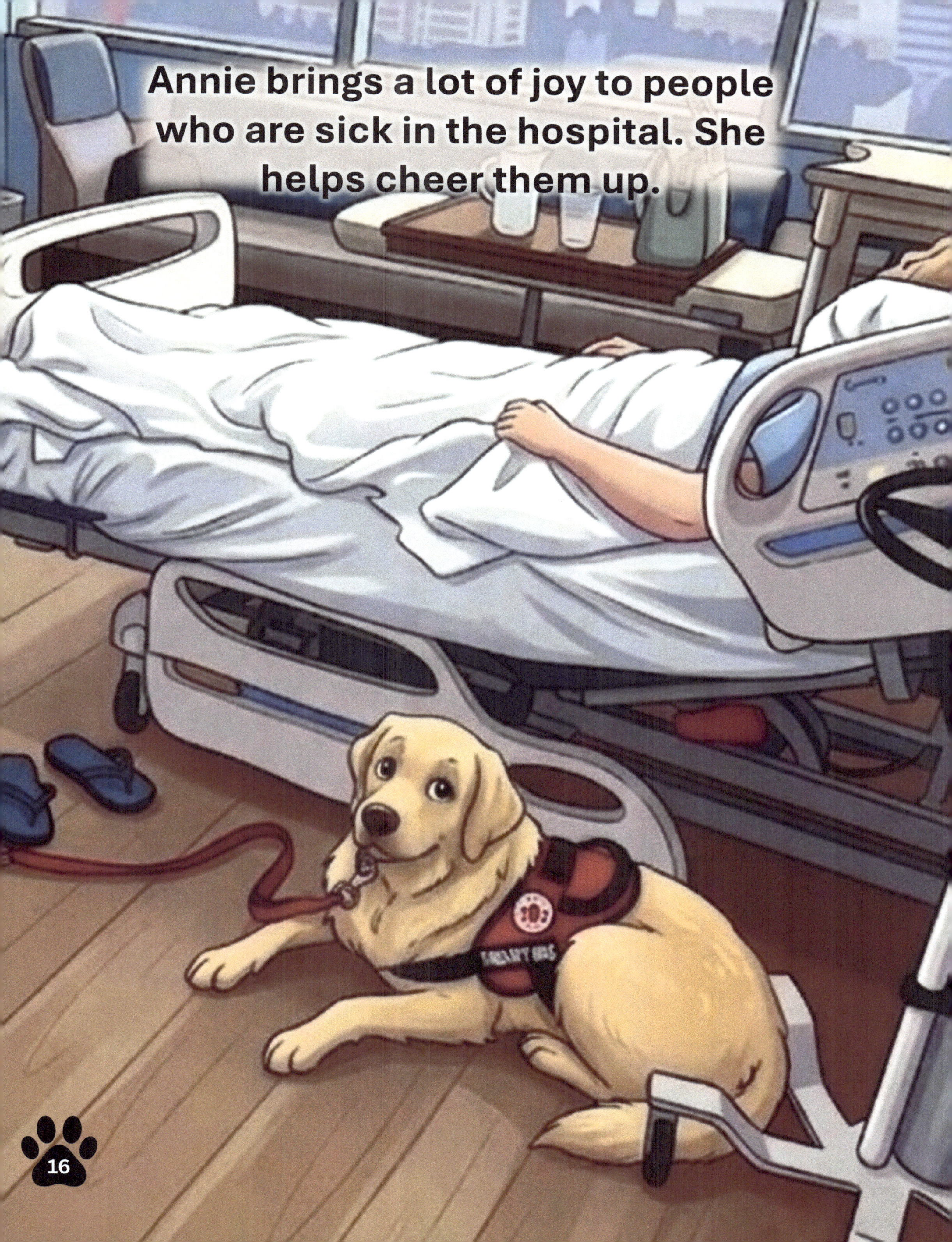

Annie brings a lot of joy to people who are sick in the hospital. She helps cheer them up.
16

Annie sometimes helps in hospitals. She will hop up on the patient's bed to give comfort.

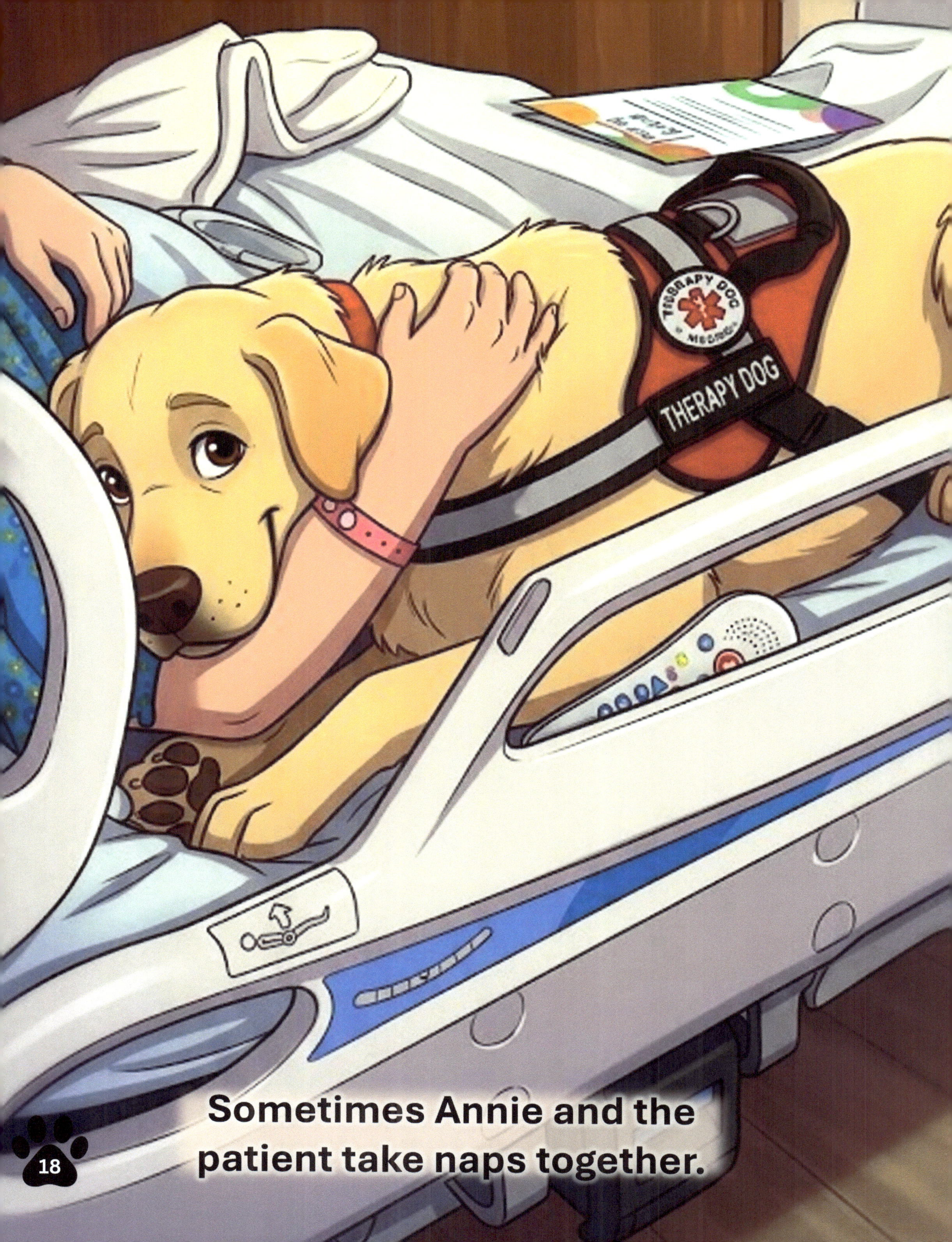

Sometimes Annie and the patient take naps together.

Wow! Long day. Time to go to sleep, so she can play in the mountains for the weekend.
LunePet
19

Annie likes to take hikes in the snow
with the crisp, fresh mountain air.

Annie plays and runs in the snow. The deeper the better!

Sometimes she wears her doggy goggles when her humans take her snowshoeing.

Annie loves to play in the snow with her human. They are going to make snow angels.

When Annie is not working, she enjoys hikes in the Colorado mountains too.

Here, Annie found a beautiful grove
of Columbines. The Columbine is
Colorado's state flower.

25

Annie also likes to swim and play in the mountain rivers and lakes. The rivers are very cold from the snow melt but that doesn't seem to bother her.

What a fun weekend! Annie is rested and ready to go back to work making people comfortable and happy at the dental office.

uchealth
HIGHLANDS RANCH HOSPITAL
1500 Park Central Drive

Annie

This is a true story about Annie the Therapy Dog. Who in real life is a working dog who comforts patients in a dental office and hospitals. Annie is a English Yellow Labrador Retriever. She works full-time in a dental office in Highlands Ranch, Colorado. Annie has become famous for laying in people's laps during dental procedures. Which has been shown to lower blood pressure and dental anxiety. Annie has viral videos on TikTok and Instagram with thousands of followers and has caught the eye of ABC 7 News in Denver, San Diego, Los Angeles, Chicago, New York and Australia. I hope you enjoy this uplifting and touching story about Annie the Therapy Dog. Visit Annie the Therapy Dog @funny.bunny9215.

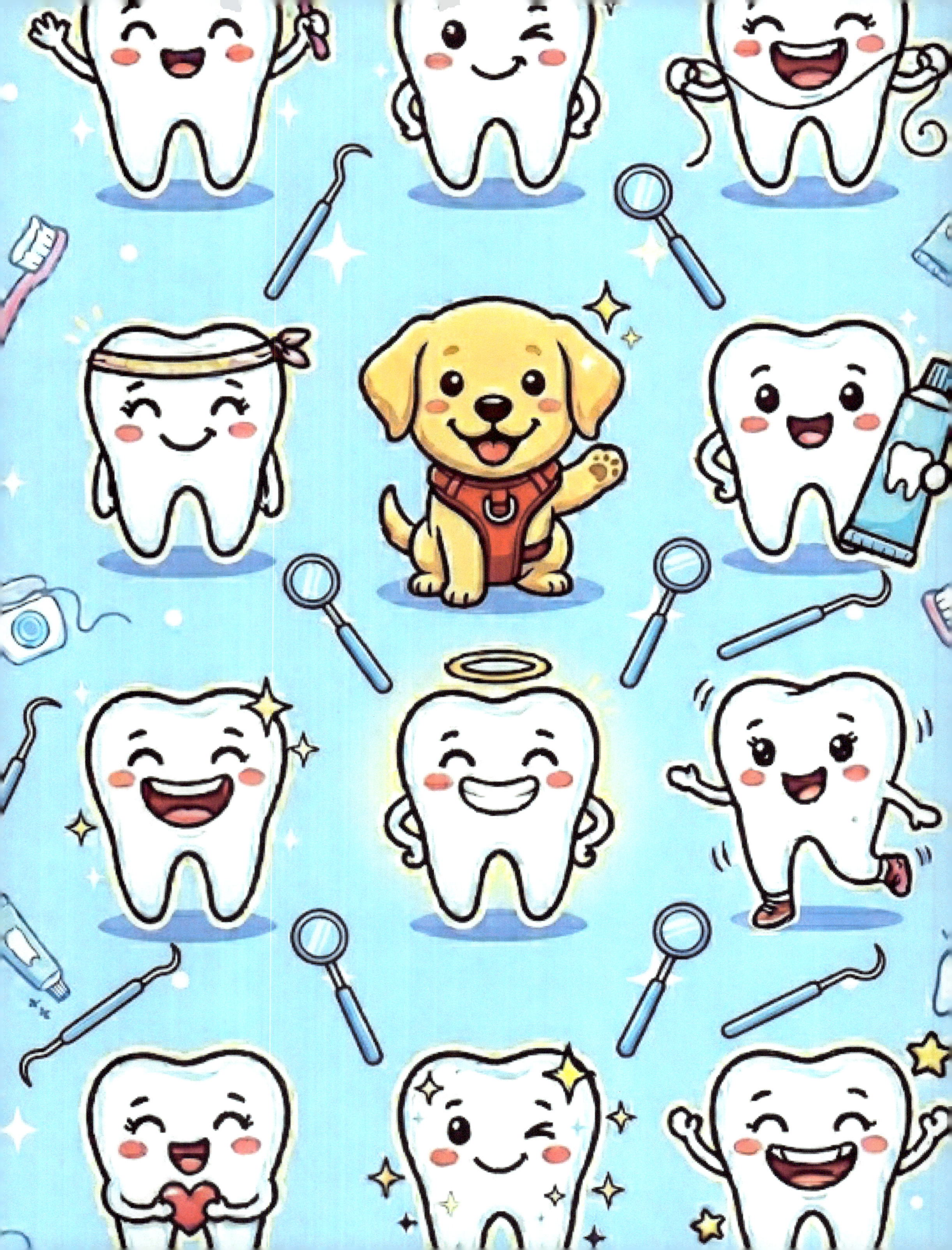

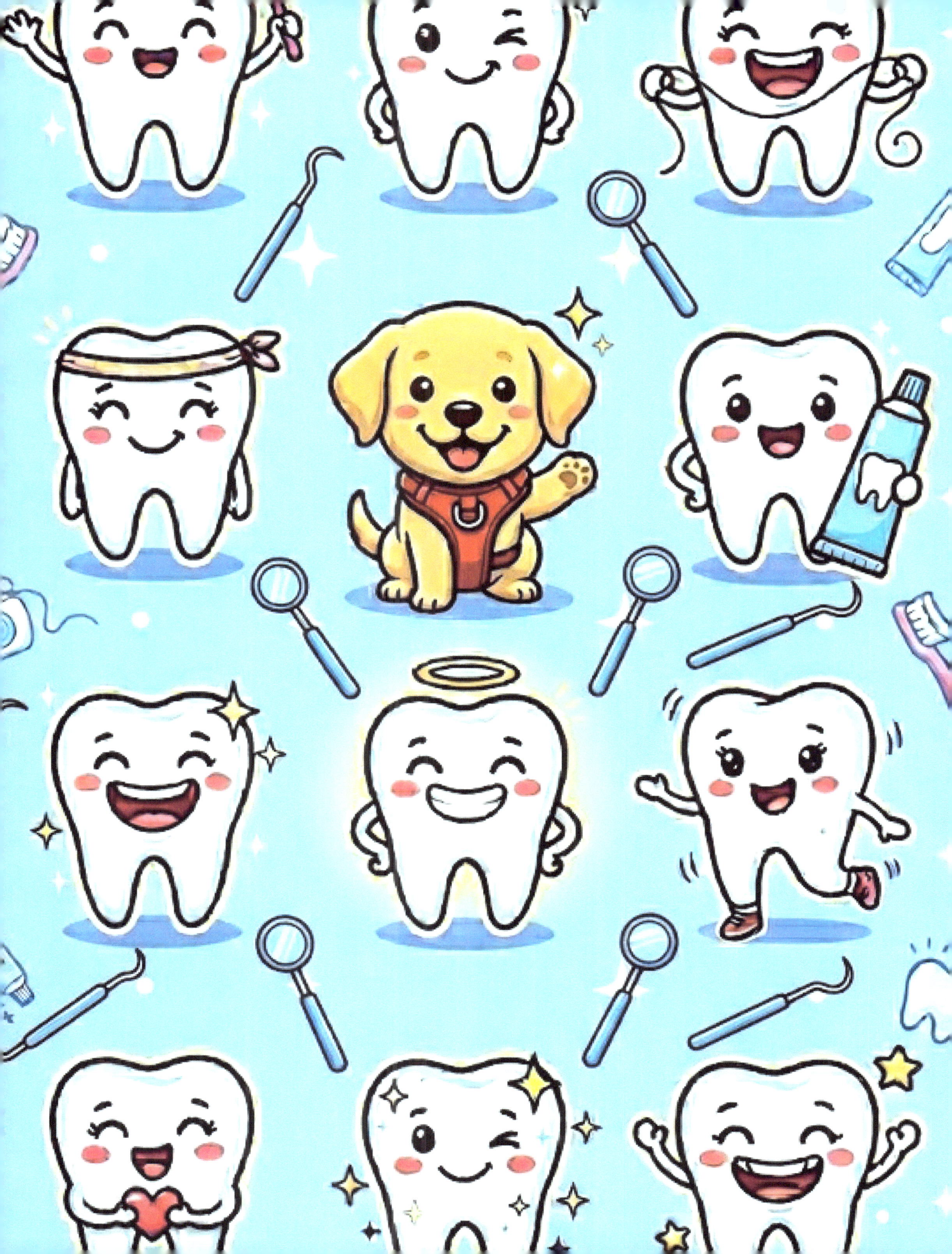